Stephen KING

MASTER OF HORROR

Anne Saidman

Lerner Publications Company

Minneapolis

This book is available in two editions:
Library binding by Lerner Publications Company
Soft cover by First Avenue Editions
241 First Avenue North
Minneapolis, Minnesota 55401

For my son, Matthew, who loves books—A. S.

LIBRARY OF CONGRESS CATALOGING-IN-PUBLICATION DATA

Saidman, Anne.
   Stephen King / by Anne Saidman.
      p.   cm.   —(The Achievers)
   Summary: Traces the life of a popular novelist, from his child-
hood as an avid reader to his current success as a creator of horror
fiction.
   ISBN 0-8225-0545-2 (lib. bdg.)
   ISBN 0-8225-9623-7 (pbk.)
   1. King, Stephen, 1947-   —Juvenile literature. 2. Novelists,
American—20th century—Biography—Juvenile literature. 3. Hor-
ror tales, American—History and criticism—Juvenile literature.
[1. King, Stephen, 1947-   . 2. Authors, American.] I. Title.
II. Series.
PS3561.I483Z87   1992
813'.54—dc20
[B]   91-26082
                                 CIP
                                  AC

Manufactured in the United States of America

International Standard Book Number: 0-8225-0545-2 (lib. bdg.)
International Standard Book Number: 0-8225-9623-7 (pbk.)
Library of Congress Catalog Number:

1 2 3   4 5 6 7 8 9 10 01 00 99 98 97 96 95 94 93 92

Contents

1 Reading and Writing 7

2 One After Another 19

3 Firestarter 27

4 More Horror 33

5 Too Many Books 39

6 Moving On 45

  Bibliography 54

David, 7, Stephen, 5, and their mother, Ruth.

1

Reading and Writing

Stephen King and his wife, Tabitha, were celebrating. It was 1973, and Stephen's book *Carrie* was going to be published; Stephen was going to be paid $2,500.00. It seemed like a lot of money to them—they had bills to pay, and the telephone had been turned off. They didn't know that in just a few years, Stephen's books would be worth millions.

Stephen had been born in Portland, Maine, on September 21, 1947. His father, Donald, deserted the family when Stephen was young. To make up for not having a father, Stephen invented a daredevil named Cannonball Cannon who "did good deeds." Stephen's mother took on a variety of low-paying jobs to support Stephen and his older brother and moved the family to Durham, Maine, so she could take care of her aging parents.

Stephen's father had left behind a collection of paperback books—all fantasy-horror fiction—that included the works of H. P. Lovecraft. Stephen found the books, and they excited him. He also found several horror stories that his father had written and submitted, unsuccessfully, to various magazines.

Stephen was a tall, lonely child who wore thick glasses and was often picked last for team sports. His hobbies were listening to horror stories on the radio and reading scary comic books, like *Weird Science, Tales From the Crypt,* and *Tales From the Vault.* He also enjoyed science fiction movies that had monsters in them, such as *Invasion of the Body Snatchers, Creature From the Black Lagoon, The Thing,* and *It Came From Outer Space.* He remembers seeing *Creature From the Black Lagoon* when he was five or six years old and saying, "This is good, I like this. This is really nice."

Stephen was an avid reader, and he enjoyed a wide variety of books. He liked detective stories by John D. MacDonald and Ed McBain, Shirley Jackson's *We Have Always Lived in the Castle* and *The Haunting of Hill House,* and J. R. R. Tolkien's *The Lord of the Rings* trilogy. He read Ken Kesey's *One Flew Over the Cuckoo's Nest* and Margaret Mitchell's *Gone with the Wind,* as well as everything he could find by Robert Howard, Andre Norton, Jack London, Agatha Christie, and Margaret Millar. In addition, he read the novels of Thomas Hardy, an English author he says influenced him greatly.

The *Creature from the Black Lagoon*

In *Invasion of the Body Snatchers,* friends anguish over a recent snatchee.

Somewhere along the way, Stephen decided he would be a writer. By the time he was in high school, he was writing offbeat short stories and sending them to science fiction magazines. None of those stories were published, but he did win first prize in a magazine essay contest. He also played tackle on the school football team and guitar with a rock-and-roll band.

He disliked many of the books he was assigned to read in school, such as Melville's *Moby Dick,* but he continued to read on his own. He remembers reading Richard Matheson's novel *The Shrinking Man* and other works that were adapted for "The Twilight Zone" on television, as well as *Peyton Place* and *Kings Row,* books about small-town society. He began to sense that he could write in a way that would combine his small-town background with his love of horror. He also developed his style, beginning his stories with things that are familiar and reassuring, such as superhighways and small-town high schools. Soon vague, small oddities begin to appear, followed by full-scale horror. Usually, good people suffer and evil-doers are destroyed.

After high school, Stephen received a scholarship to attend the University of Maine at Orono. He majored in English and wrote a weekly column called "King's Garbage Truck" for the college newspaper, and he also earned extra money working as a dishwasher, Little League coach, and gas station attendant.

In one of his creative writing classes, Stephen met his future wife, Tabitha Jane Spruce.

Stephen was a serious writer even as a teenager.

In 1967, Stephen's story "The Glass Floor" was bought for $35.00 by *Startling Mystery Stories* magazine. It was his first professionally published work of fiction. By the time Stephen graduated from college in 1970, he had sold another short story, "The Reaper's Image," to the same magazine for the same price. Over the next few years, more of his stories were published in magazines like *Cavalier, Gent, Penthouse, Cosmopolitan,* and *Adam,* but Stephen received very little money for them. He wanted to teach, but he couldn't find a teaching job, so he worked at a launderette for $60.00 a week.

On January 2, 1971, Stephen and Tabitha got married. Stephen was still working at the launderette, and they were very poor. In fact, Stephen walked down the aisle in a suit, tie, and shoes that he had borrowed. He says, "We got married on a Saturday because the place [the launderette] was closed on Saturday afternoons.... Everyone wished me well, but I still was docked for not being in that Saturday morning."

Stephen finally found a job at the Hampden Academy, a private coeducational secondary school in Hampden, Maine, where he taught high school English for $6,000 a year. He went on writing short stories whenever he had time, and he began to work on a book.

Meanwhile, Stephen and Tabitha had their first child, a daughter named Naomi. Stephen continued to sell stories to magazines once in a while. He remembers that the payment for the stories "always seemed to come just in time to buy antibiotics for the baby's ear infection or to keep the telephone in the apartment for another record-breaking month."

Then the Kings had another baby, a son they named Joe. There was barely enough money for food, and none for the telephone. Stephen felt that his writing wasn't paying enough, and he become so discouraged that he threw his book manuscript away. Luckily, Tabitha pulled it out of the garbage. She persuaded Stephen to send it to William Thompson, an editor at Doubleday who had shown an interest in him. Doubleday decided to publish the book, which was called *Carrie*. The title came from a book that Stephen had read, Theodore Dreiser's *Sister Carrie*. Appropriately, Stephen dedicated it to Tabitha.

Carrie is the story of a lonely high school girl who is tormented by her classmates and her mother. Stephen said that the book "tries to deal with the loneliness of one girl, her desperate effort to become a part of the peer society in which she must exist, and how her effort fails." He admitted that he had drawn on his own childhood and small-town background while writing the novel. Carrie has telekinetic powers—the ability to move objects just by using her mind. When she is humiliated at the prom, she uses those powers to destroy the town and get back at her enemies.

14

Carrie (Sissy Spacek) and Tommy (William Katt), queen and king of the senior prom, in *Carrie,* the movie based on Stephen King's novel of the same name

Stephen's beard is seasonal. He often lets it grow from the end of the World Series until the beginning of baseball spring training in Florida.

Doubleday released *Carrie* in April of 1974. Later that year, Stephen described his reaction when his editor at Doubleday told him that the paperback rights to *Carrie* had been sold: "I thought he was going to tell me I was only getting $5,000 or something. He said $400,000. The only thing I could think to do was go out and buy my wife a hair dryer. I stumbled across the street to get it and thought I would probably get greased by some car."

Many critics complained that *Carrie* was gory and overdone, but horror fans loved it. After the book had been in paperback for just nine months, there were over one million copies of it in print. However, Stephen himself did not like the book and thought of it as just some old thing he had put together.

In 1976 *Carrie* was made into a movie, directed by Brian De Palma and starring Sissy Spacek. It became one of the highest money-making films of the year. Another paperback edition of the book was published to tie in with the film, and over four million copies were sold. Stephen says that "the movie made the book and the book made me."

Stephen and Tabitha refused to let their children see *Carrie* when it was released. Stephen explained, "The movie and the book have uncomfortable things to say about parents who hate their children and use them, and about children who are put upon by their peer groups. We thought it would be upsetting." Naomi did eventually read the book, but after that she refused to read any of her father's later works.

After the huge success of *Carrie,* Stephen stopped working as a teacher and became a full-time author. His extraordinary career had begun.

Someone (or something) from the film *Salem's Lot*

2

One After Another

Stephen never changed his opinion of *Carrie*, but he said that "what the book did do was give me a little running room to write a better book, which was *Salem's Lot*."

Salem's Lot is about what happens when vampires take over a small town in Maine. Stephen got the idea for it while he was teaching Bram Stoker's *Dracula* at the Hampden Academy. He had begun to think about the types of problems that vampires would face in the contemporary United States.

Salem's Lot was another big success. After just six months, there were two million copies of the book in print. In 1979 it was made into a successful television miniseries, directed by Tobe Hooper, who had become famous for directing *The Texas Chainsaw Massacre*. Stephen continued to write.

In 1983, Stephen talks with Kareem Abdul-Jabbar on the set of *Pet Sematary.*

His third book, which was published in 1977, was *The Shining.* It tells what happens when a writer and his wife are the winter caretakers of an isolated, haunted hotel in Colorado. Their young son has the ability to "shine," or see things that other people can't. The hotel looks empty, but its rooms are occupied by numerous ghosts that the boy can see. Stephen got the idea for the book while he was at a fashionable resort in Colorado on the last day of the tourist season.

Richard Lingeman reviewed *The Shining* for the *New York Times,* praising Stephen's writing. He called Stephen "a natural," but added that "he lacks control; he simply rears back and lets fly with the fireball, and a lot of wild pitches result." Other reviewers complained that the book was heavy-handed and muddled. Stephen himself called it "a very nasty, dark book." Despite the negative reviews, which often don't reflect a book's popularity, *The Shining* was another success.

Stephen was growing unhappy with Doubleday, his publishing company. The $2,500 advance that he had received for *Carrie* was a good amount for a first novel. But even after his books were earning millions of dollars, Doubleday's advances were relatively small. In addition, Stephen was not being treated well by the Doubleday management. According to William Thompson, Stephen's editor at Doubleday, "Every time he came to the office, I'd have to introduce him all over again to the executives." Eventually Stephen left Doubleday and signed with New American Library, which had offered him a $2.5 million contract for three novels. New American Library would publish the paperback version of his books, while Viking would publish them in hardcover.

In 1980 Warner Brothers made a movie version of *The Shining,* directed by Stanley Kubrick. Stephen was unhappy with the film. He complained, "Stanley

Kubrick's stated purpose was to make a horror picture, and I don't think he understood. . . ." The film, which was advertised as "the ultimate horror movie," was not a big success.

Meanwhile, Stephen had written two more books, which were both published in 1978. One was *The Stand,* about a deadly superflu; the other was *Night Shift,* a collection of bizarre short stories. He also was a writer-in-residence at the University of Maine during the 1978–79 school year. During that time, Stephen's third child was born, a son named Owen.

The King family had been living in Lovell, a small town in Maine with a population of about 600 people. In 1979 the Kings purchased a second home in Bangor, Maine, where they planned to live for most of the year. Stephen explained, "It got kind of sad to see our kids just playing with each other and not having much in the way of companionship. Also, I got tired of making an eight-mile drive for [supplies]."

Their new home was 150 miles from where Stephen grew up. Although the Kings could have afforded to live anywhere, they preferred to remain in the small-town world they knew. According to Stephen, "Maine is far and away better for a couple of hicks like us, and it's better for the kids."

The family's new house was actually a 23-room, 129-year-old mansion. Stephen and Tabitha installed a black iron fence, with a bat-and-spider-web design.

It was rumored that the house was haunted by a previous owner named General Weber, who had died in the house after saying, "I'm not leaving." A stable on the property was remodeled into a study for Stephen to write in, and the Kings also added an indoor, solar-heated swimming pool.

23

Stephen's next book was *The Dead Zone,* published in 1979. It is about a young man who wakes
up from a four-year coma with second sight. The man,
who is able to see into the future, knows that a leading
politician will become a dictator.

The Dead Zone was made into a film that was released in October of 1983. The movie did well, and so did the book, which stayed on the *New York Times* best-seller list for six months. By the time it came off the list, Stephen had written another book.

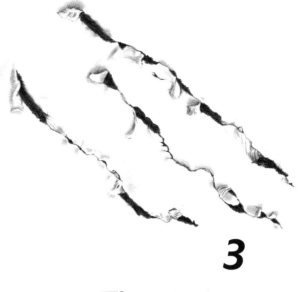

3

Firestarter

Stephen's next book was *Firestarter*. It is about what happens when two college students who are part of a government experiment have a daughter with a unique gift, the ability to make objects catch on fire just by using her mind. The family is pursued by a dangerous government agency that wants to use the girl's ability as a weapon.

Firestarter came out in 1980. That same year, Stephen had three different books on the *New York Times* best-seller lists at the same time. While *Firestarter* was on the hardcover best-seller list, *The Dead Zone* and *The Shining* were on the paperback best-seller list.

Firestarter was made into a movie in 1983. People who lived near the location of the film's shooting in Wilmington, North Carolina, offered to sell their homes to be burned down in the movie. The film starred George C. Scott and Martin Sheen, with Drew Barrymore, from *E.T.*, as the girl. She had read the book and told her mother she wanted the role. Drew explained, "I thought it would be neat to see all these fires and effects. I set a lot of people on fire, but they deserve it." The movie version of *Firestarter* was filled with eye-popping special effects, such as fireballs racing toward the viewer and human torches, and it ended with a gigantic fire.

Stephen also got some bad news in 1980—his health was not good, and his weight had been climbing. He began taking six-mile hikes to work off the weight, and over the years he has continued to use long walks as his major source of exercise.

In 1981 Stephen's novel *Cujo* was published. It is the story of a formerly gentle dog that contracts rabies and terrorizes a small town. The book suggests that the dog is possessed by the ghost of a mass murderer.

Christopher Lehmann-Haupt, who reviewed *Cujo* for the *New York Times*, called it Stephen's "cruelest, most disturbing" book yet. Stephen himself admitted that it was "a very dark book," although he did point out that there was still hope for the characters that survived.

Cujo was another success, climbing to the top of the *New York Times* best-seller list within days of its

From *Firestarter,* Art Carney and Louise Fletcher in back; and Drew Barrymore and David Keith in front.

publication. By then there were over 22 million copies of Stephen's various books in print.

Stephen published a second book in 1981. It was *Danse Macabre,* which he described as "an informal overview" of horror in radio, television, and film. That same year, he also worked on the movie *Creepshow* with George Romero, who had directed *The Night of the Living Dead,* a cult classic. Stephen said that the idea behind *Creepshow* was "simply to put people in movie theaters and see if we can scare hell out of them. I want people crawling under the seats with popcorn and jujubes in their hair."

Stephen relives his days as a teenager in a rock band.

That same year, Stephen's wife, Tabitha, wrote *Small World*, a novel. The book was about a mad scientist and was published by Macmillan. She received $165,000 for the paperback rights, an unusually large amount for a first novel. Tabitha knew that her being Stephen King's wife had helped the book's sales. She said, "I put ten years into helping his career, so if his name helps me with mine, I think it's [fair]." Her book was dedicated to Stephen. The inscription read, "For the bogeyman, with love."

Stephen was surprised. He said, "I knew she could write poetry, but I never guessed she could write such a good novel right out of the box." He admitted, "Deep down, I may have been a little jealous, with a small voice saying, 'Hey, wait a minute. That's my toy.'" Tabitha laughed at the suggestion that she might pull Stephen's readers away. She said, "I'd be nuts to compete with him."

It was a good year for the Kings, and there was more to follow.

From *Creepshow*, the Creep

4

More Horror

By 1982 there were over 25 million copies of Stephen's books in print, and many of his novels had been translated into foreign languages. That same year, his book *Different Seasons* was published, his tenth book in eight years. *Different Seasons* is actually a collection of short novels, only one of which caused the scary chills that usually accompanied a Stephen King book. One of the stories is called "The Body." It is about a group of 12-year-old boys who search for a missing friend and was used as the basis for the 1986 film *Stand By Me. Different Seasons* was actually Stephen's attempt to be recognized as more than just a writer of horror stories. He said, "I've worked on it harder than anything I've ever done."

One critic complained that most of Stephen's characters, in *Different Seasons* as well as in his other books, talk as though they spend all their time watching movies and television. Another critic described the book as a dazzling display of how writing can appeal to people who don't normally like to read. The many mixed reviews did not keep the book from becoming another best-selling success.

The movie *Creepshow* was released late in October of 1982. A comic book version of the script was published as well. *Creepshow* was so successful that Stephen began working on a sequel.

The following year, two more books of Stephen's were published, *Pet Sematary* and *Christine. Pet Sematary,* about strange happenings at a graveyard, was so disturbing to Stephen that he left it in a drawer for a while when it was finished. In fact, it bothered him so much that in 1984 he refused an offer of $1 million for the movie rights. In 1985, however, he worked out a deal with George Romero to film the book. Stephen received $1,000 in advance, along with an agreement that made him a financial and creative partner in the movie. According to Romero, the deal was arranged because "Steve felt the movie was in friendly hands."

Stephen's second book in 1983 was *Christine,* about a teenager's obsession with his car, which is possessed by the ghost of a previous owner.

Stephen as Jordy Verrill in *Creepshow*

The title car chases a high-school bully in *Christine*.

Film producer Richard Kobritz read *Christine* and bought the movie rights for $500,000. Before the filming began, people were sent to used car lots in various states to look for a 1958 Plymouth Fury. The car was actually played by 24 different automobiles, only three of which were still in one piece when the movie was finished.

The film version of *Christine* was a big hit. It was released in December of 1983, and by early January it had grossed over $10 million. Moviegoers liked it, and so did Stephen. He said, "I wanted to go back and see it over again."

Of course, there was even more still ahead.

Stephen portrayed a Christian minister in *Pet Sematary*.

5

Too Many Books

Stephen embarked on a new project in 1983. He decided to work with another horror writer, Peter Straub. The two authors had known each other since 1978. According to Stephen, "We liked each other so well that we started talking about a collaboration the second time we met."

When an interviewer asked why the two authors had decided to write together, Stephen answered, "I was intensely curious to see the result. Working together was like that ad where one guy says, 'You got chocolate on my peanut butter,' and the other guy says, 'You got peanut butter on my chocolate,' and they end up saying, 'Hey! This tastes pretty good.'"

Stephen was living in Maine, and Peter Straub's home was in Connecticut. Stephen explained how they were able to write a book together while living in different states: "We wrote the beginning and ending together. Peter put on some jazz in his office, and I wrote for a while as he read magazines. When I was done, he'd pick it up where I had left off. For the rest of the book, we divided the work. I'd write a chunk for a month or so at my house, and then Peter would continue another chunk at his."

The result of the joint effort was *The Talisman,* a fantasy about a 12-year-old boy's journey through a world filled with vicious werewolves and killer trees.

People were curious about which parts of the book had been written by which author, but neither would tell. Straub said, "We're never going to answer that. But I can tell you that when people guess, they're usually wrong."

An interviewer asked if they had argued about how the book should proceed. "Not at all," Stephen answered. "Except Peter thinks a computer is great to write on, and I'm less enraptured. It makes me feel like I'm in the James Bond movie where he's tied to an exercise machine. Peter's a friend and I only have about three of them. He makes me laugh harder than anyone else."

"That's because you're twisted," Peter replied.

The Talisman was released in November of 1984 and quickly became the number-one best-selling book. Stephen told a reporter that he thought the book was so popular because "It's more fun to read a fantasy like this at night than to sit around thinking, 'Oh, I've got to go to work tomorrow, and my boss is so ugly.'" Steven Spielberg, who had directed *E.T.*, immediately bought the film rights. *The Talisman* had a first printing of 600,000 copies. It was a record number at the time, although many of Stephen's later works surpassed it.

Some critics complained that the book had so many movie-type special effects that it seemed to have been written specifically for film, but Stephen denied it. He said, "Why would anyone who's done as well writing books as Peter or me ever stoop to the idea of selling a movie scenario as a novel? The word 'film' never crossed our lips when we wrote."

Two other major events occurred in Stephen's life in 1984. The film *Children of the Corn,* based on one of his short stories, appeared, and he bought a radio station in Bangor. He likes to write his books while listening to rock music, and the local rock station, WZON, was having financial problems. The station's owners wanted to switch from rock music to another format. In order to prevent that from happening, Stephen purchased the station himself. He has since sold it.

Stephen is a compulsive writer; he turns out about 1,500 words a day, no matter where he is. The only days he takes off are his birthday, the Fourth of July, and Christmas. In fact, the enormous amount of material that he produces had become a problem, because most publishers don't want to publish more than one book a year by a major author. For that reason, Stephen wrote and published five novels under another name, Richard Bachman. However, readers quickly discovered that Bachman was actually Stephen King. He grumbled, "It should have been in *Time* [magazine's] milestones. Died. Richard Bachman, of cancer of the pseudonym." *The Running Man,* one of the books he wrote as Richard Bachman, was adapted into a movie starring Arnold Schwarzenegger.

Stephen's next book was *Skeleton Crew,* a collection of short stories published in 1985. It was followed in 1986 by another book, *It,* which tells the story of a group of children who fight a monster in the sewers of their hometown in the 1950s. Thirty years later, they have grown up and some of them have moved away. They come together when the monster reappears, and they fight it once again.

Stephen explained how he constructed the story: "I've written the book in two parallel lines: the story of what they did as kids and the story of what they're doing as grown-ups. That's what I mean when I say I'm interested in the notion of finishing off one's childhood as one completes making a wheel. The idea is to come back and confront your childhood, in a sense relive it if you can, so that you can be whole."

It was very long—1,138 pages—but the length did not take away from its popularity. Although Stephen said *It* was "very badly constructed," the book became a best-seller, and by October 1986 there were 1,025,000 copies of *It* in print. Altogether, there were more than 60 million copies of his books in print.

Robert Gould, a New York City psychiatrist, tried to explain why Stephen's books, and horror stories in general, were so popular. He said that horror "is extremely distracting.... In difficult times, in the world outside and your own world, you reach out far from yourself. Also, you can control that horror. You can stop reading anytime you want."

Stephen added, "Deep inside, most of us entertain fears, even if it's in the middle of the night. Certainly we fear being hurt, either emotionally or physically. There has to be some artistic way to cope with those fears."

He admits that he has many fears of his own: "I'm afraid the world may blow up. It's like my fear of flying. Flying scares me because I'm not in control of the situation." He adds, "On a more personal level, I don't like the dark very much. I'm nervous when I don't know where my kids are. I suppose they're the same fears anybody has, but I write about them." He has also said that he is scared of spiders, elevators, sewers, funerals, cancer, black cats, and walking under ladders.

Stephen wanted to write other types of books, and he insisted that *It* would be his last horror novel. He said, "For now, as far as the Stephen King Book-of-the-Month Club goes, this is the clearance-sale time. Everything must go."

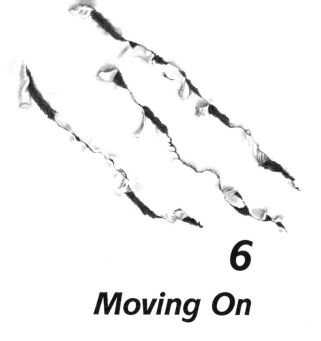

6

Moving On

Stephen was part of a new trend—recording books onto audio cassettes. One of the first such recordings was planned for Stephen's book *Night Shift*. He also continued to write books, one after another.

In 1986 Stephen's novel *Misery,* about a crazed nurse who captures her favorite writer, was published. Before long it was made into a movie, directed by Rob Reiner. In 1987 Stephen's *Tommyknockers,* a science fiction epic, came out. Stephen said, "It's about how our ability to make gadgets outraces [our sense of right and wrong]." The book had a first printing of one million copies. In 1990, *It* was shown as a miniseries on television and was widely viewed by an audience that had come to look forward to anything bearing the name of Stephen King.

With as many fans as Stephen King has, book signings are hard work.

In October 1990, Stephen's book *Four Past Midnight,* consisting of four short novels, was published. The next month, the film version of *Misery* was released and received excellent reviews. Another film that came out around the same time, *Tales from the Darkside: The Movie,* contained a section based on one of Stephen's short stories, "Cat from Hell."

In the winter of 1989-90, Stephen had a record of five books on the hardcover and paperback best-seller lists of the *New York Times.* By January 1991, there were over 89 million copies of his books in paperback alone. He was earning millions of dollars for each book he wrote, and he was the best-selling author in two foreign countries—Germany and Sweden.

Stephen, who describes his novels as "the literary equivalent of a Big Mac and a large fries from McDonald's," attributes his success to hard work and practice. He explains it as "a matter of exercise. If you work out with weights for 15 minutes a day over a course of 10 years, you're gonna get muscles. If you write for an hour and a half [a day] for 10 years, you're gonna turn into a good writer."

Stephen has a seemingly inexhaustible imagination. Even critics who think that he does not write well admit that they have been spellbound by his ability to tell a story. Many critics seem to praise Stephen grudgingly, as if they want to criticize him at the same time. For example, Walter Kendrick wrote in

The Village Voice: "There's unmistakeable genius in Stephen King, and though it's genius of a trivial kind...still it's [matchless]." Another example of this mixed criticism came from John Podhoretz, who wrote about Stephen in the *Wall Street Journal:* "He manages to create characters who, while never convincing, nonetheless interest and move us."

Stephen understands the two-sided nature of the criticism. He feels that society is obsessed by the dark side of life that he writes about, and yet that same society doesn't consider this type of writing to be real literature. He says, "People ask me, 'When are you going to write something serious?' A question like that always hurts." He adds, "My answer is that I'm as serious as I can be every time I sit down at a typewriter."

Stephen's books always involve children. He explains, "They just pop up. They always have, from the time I was a kid, writing as a kid. They seem to represent a whole range of really romantic notions. They [represent] the powers of good. They're clear-eyed. They're very useful in fantasy because they have a broad spectrum of perceptions."

When Stephen was asked if he used his own children in his books, he answered: "Sure, although probably I think more about what I remember from my own childhood than I do about them. But, for instance, Charlie McGee, in *Firestarter,* was very consciously patterned on my daughter, because I know how she looks, I know how she walks. I know what makes her mad. I was able to use that, but only to a certain degree. Beyond that, if you tie yourself to your own children, you limit your range. So I took Naomi, used her as the frame, and then went where I wanted."

Despite Stephen's multi-million-dollar success, the King family lives modestly for millionaires. Stephen dresses simply, usually in blue jeans. The King children have an Atari game, and Stephen owns a VCR and a giant-screen TV console. Stephen and Tabitha own several cars as well. Stephen explains, "You see, I am my work to a large extent. Work takes most of the energy. It's what gives me pleasure. It is the toy. I don't feel the need to fill up my life with tape decks and amplifiers. It's nice, but I can take it or leave it."

In many ways, Stephen has not been affected by his wealth and fame. He says, "Nothing really changes. I'll still be told by my wife, 'Steve, we need a loaf of bread,' and so I'll go out shopping. And if I forget, and come back instead with an idea that I tell her will make us $2 million, she'll still say, 'Steve, I'm delighted, but we still need a loaf of bread.'"

Stephen's son Owen plays Little League baseball, and Stephen wrote a nonfiction article about Little League that was printed in *New Yorker* magazine in 1990. In 1991 Stephen donated $1 million to his hometown of Bangor, Maine, so that the city could build a new baseball field for its Little League teams.

That same year, another book of Stephen's, called *Needful Things,* was published. Set in the mythical town of Castle Rock, Maine, it tells about a mysterious shop owner who plays deadly tricks on the townspeople. Stephen also began writing the script for a television show to be called "Stephen King's Golden Years."

Stephen likes to spend his time in Maine and rarely leaves the state. He hates to fly. Despite the many films that have been based on his books, he tries to visit Hollywood as little as possible. He explains, "It's really strange out there. Every time I go, I feel like I should take my passport." When he has to make a business trip to New York, he eats fast food rather than dining in a fancy restaurant. His conferences with his editors usually take place at Yankee Stadium, with Stephen discussing his books amidst hot dogs and beer.

Stephen enjoys simple pleasures: bowling, swimming, cross-country skiing, and baseball. He also reads, and some of the books he has enjoyed as an adult include Mark Twain's *The Adventures of Huckleberry Finn* and Charles Dickens's *Oliver Twist,* as well as Shakespeare's *Hamlet.* He also likes the poetry of Emily Dickinson. He spends a lot of time talking with Tabitha, whom he considers to be his best friend.

Stephen delivered a commencement address and was awarded an honorary degree in May 1987.

Stephen and Tabitha's lives are bound up with their children, and one of the things they have done with their money is to make sure the children's educations are provided for. Their daughter Naomi, an avid reader and college student, hopes to be a teacher. Their son Joe, who likes horror books and hopes to be a writer like his father, is also a college student. Younger son Owen, whose room is decorated with superhero and space adventure posters, seems the most like his father, enjoying the gory parts of movies the most. The children earn their allowances by taping books for Stephen to listen to while he drives. Some of the things they have taped for him are detective novels and stories by John Steinbeck.

The Kings have a staff of four people, whose main function is to perform services so that both Stephen and Tabitha have time to write. They have a housekeeper five days a week, two secretaries, and a caretaker.

The family eats dinner together, and the conversation ranges from Little League to books, movies, and local gossip. Everyone helps out with chores on the weekend. At those times, Stephen likes to bake. He says, "I don't particularly care for sweets myself, but if I make bread or coffee cake, someone around here'll eat it."

Stephen and Tabitha usually get up every morning at 6:00 A.M. and spend several hours writing at home. Tabitha has written three books. One she calls a "political romance," one is about a Maine woman who is attacked by bullies, and one is a love story. Stephen and Tabitha have different attitudes toward their writing. Tabitha says, "Writing is only the frosting on my cake. I'm whole without it." Stephen, on the other hand, says, "Writing is what God put me on earth to do."

One of the most amazing things about Stephen King is how he has remained modest despite his success. "I've had about three original ideas in my life.... I sense the limitations of where my talents are," he says. And he insists that he has only "a small amount of talent."

Stephen has no plans to stop turning out books that people love to read. He says, "I'll always write because that's what I do best." Luckily for Stephen King fans, that means there will be other books to look forward to for years to come.

Bibliography

"A Mild Down-Easter Discovers Terror Is the Ticket." *People*, December 29, 1980 — January 5, 1981, p. 53.

Bandler, Michael J. "The King of the Macabre at Home." *Parents*, January 1982, p. 68.

Donovan, Mark. "For Years, Stephen King's *Firestarter* Was Wife Tabitha; Now She Burns to Write, Too." *People*, May 18, 1981, p. 81.

Foltz, Kim. "An Unstoppable Thriller King." *Newsweek*, June 10, 1985, p. 62.

Goldstein, Bill. "King of Horror." *Publishers Weekly*, January 24, 1991, p. 6.

Gray, Paul. "Master of Postliterate Prose." *Time*, August 30, 1982, p. 87.

Kanfer, Stefan. "King of Horror." *Time*, October 6, 1986, p. 74.

"King, Stephen." *Current Biography Yearbook 1981*. New York: H.W. Wilson Co., 1982.

Small, Michael. "Peter Straub and Stephen King Team Up for Fear." *People*, January 28, 1985, p. 50.

Zoglin, Richard. "Giving Hollywood the Chills." *Time*, January 9, 1984, p. 56.

ACKNOWLEDGMENTS

Photographs are reproduced through the courtesy of: James Leonard, pp. 1, 26; Independent Picture Service, pp. 2, 6, 20, 23, 35, 46; Hollywood Book and Poster, pp. 9, 15, 18, 29, 32, 36, 38; Wisconsin Center for Film and Theater Research, p. 10; David King, p. 12; Tabitha King, p. 16, 43; Voscar, the Maine Photographer, p. 24; © Elliott Smith, p. 30; Jack Walas, University of Maine, p. 51; Photofest, p. 55; Jill Simon, p. 56.

ABOUT THE AUTHOR

Besides being a school librarian and a writer, Anne Saidman is a photographer and a juggler. She lives in Brooklyn, New York, with her husband and their son.